Marsupials

Jeanne Sturm

Rourke
Educational Media

rourkeeducationalmedia.com

Teacher Notes available at
rem4teachers.com

www.rourkeeducationalmedia.com

PHOTO CREDITS: Cover: © Craig Dingle; Title Page: © Dirk Freder; 3: © Craig Hale; Page 4: © Fby; Page 5: ©, René Lorenz, Ildogesto; Page 6: © Ron Chapple; Page 7: © Melissa Woods; Page 8: © PeteKaras; Page 9: © MaXPdia, Craig Dingle; Page 10: © Martine Oger, Craig Dingle; Page 11: © Craig Dingle, Callan Chesser; Page 12: © scibak, Isselee; Page 13: © Craig Dingle; Page 14: © Jason Gehrman, Hotshotsworldwide, Wei-chuan Liu, Ben Mcleish, Smellme, Zepherwind; Page 15: © Ian Danbury, Dean Turner, Redzaal, Frank Leung, MoMorad, Holger Mette; Page 16: © Teekaygee, John Bell; Page 17: © stock_art, Charles Schug; Page 18: © Clayton Hansen; Page 19: © Robyn Mackenzie, nimu1956; Page 20: © Keiichi Hiki ; Page 21: © Fby; Page 22: © MoMorad;

Edited by Precious McKenzie

Cover Design by Renee Brady
Interior Design by Cory Davis

Library of Congress PCN Data

Marsupials / Jeanne Sturm
(Eye to Eye with Animals)
ISBN 978-1-61810-114-3 (hard cover) (alk. paper)
ISBN 978-1-61810-247-8 (soft cover)
Library of Congress Control Number: 2011944405

Rourke Educational Media
Printed in the United States of America,
North Mankato, Minnesota

rourkeeducationalmedia.com
customerservice@rourkeeducationalmedia.com • PO Box 643328 Vero Beach, Florida 32964

Table of Contents

Chapter 1
Practical Pouches

Koalas, kangaroos, and opossums are just a few of the **mammals** that belong to a special group called marsupials. Like other mammals, marsupials give birth to live offspring. Unlike other mammals, marsupial babies are born before they are fully developed, at only 2 to 5 weeks of age. When born, the tiny babies make their way to their mother's pouch where they continue to grow and develop until they can live on their own.

Koala

Tasmanian devil

Where in the world do marsupials live?

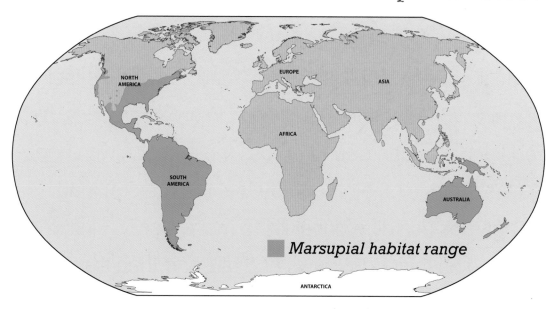

Marsupial habitat range

Most marsupial species, including the kangaroo, koala, and Tasmanian devil, live in Australia and New Zealand. More than 60 species of opossums, including the tiny mouse opossum, live in Central and South America. Only one marsupial species, the Virginia opossum, lives in North America.

Chapter 2
Boomers and Flyers

Kangaroos live in Australia. The red kangaroo is the largest of all kangaroos and the largest marsupial. Males grow to more than 6 feet (1.8 meters) tall and weigh up to 200 pounds (90 kilograms).

Kangaroos use their tails for balance while hopping and for support while standing. They can hop as fast as 40 miles (64 kilometers) per hour. In an emergency, a red kangaroo can bound across the outback with hops 10 feet (3 meters) high and 39 feet (12 meters) long. Kangaroos use different skills to move slowly. First, they balance on their front paws and tail, and then they swing their hind legs forward.

DID YOU KNOW?

A male kangaroo is called a boomer, buck, or jack. A female is a flyer, doe, or jill. A young kangaroo is called a joey.

Kangaroos are born after about 31 to 36 days **gestation**. Once it makes its way to the pouch, a baby red kangaroo will remain there for around 190 days, continuing to develop. A mother kangaroo can use muscles to control her pouch size and opening. When she is alarmed, she can pull the pouch tight to keep the young kangaroo safe inside. When the joey is between 6 and 8 months old, it will leave the pouch to explore the outside world, and then return to the pouch to sleep and nurse. At about one year old, it will leave the pouch for good.

To drink its mother's milk, the joey must find the nipple inside its mother's pouch. When the joey is small, it can nurse inside the pouch. As the joey grows bigger and stronger, it can nurse from outside the pouch.

Kangaroos are **herbivores**. They eat a wide variety of plants, including grass shoots, herbs, and leaves. They are adapted to life in Australia, where water can be scarce, and they get much of the moisture they need from green grass. When they **migrate**, their highly developed sense of smell helps them locate water sources even in times of drought.

 During extremely dry times, kangaroos will migrate as far as 125 miles (200 kilometers) to find water.

Wallabies are closely related to kangaroos. They also live in Australia.

Chapter 3
Screechers, Sleepers, and Hangers-On

Tasmanian devil

▲▲ *Tasmanian devils live on the Australian island of Tasmania.*

Tasmanian devils are the largest marsupial **carnivores**, weighing in at 8-26 pounds (4-12 kilograms). Tasmanian devils are **nocturnal**. Alert at night, they use their keen senses of smell and hearing to hunt insects, opossums, and wallabies. They are also **scavengers**, and get most of their nutrients from eating animals that have already died. With powerful jaws and sharp teeth, they rip at the hide and crush the bones of dead animals. Scavengers play an important role in their habitat. Without them, animal **carcasses** would pile up in rotten, decaying heaps.

▲
▲ *As soon as they are born, Tasmanian devil babies race to their mother's pouch. The mother has four teats inside her pouch. Only the first four babies to arrive and attach to a teat will survive.*

11

Koalas live in East Australia. They spend most of their lives in eucalyptus trees, sleeping and resting up to 18 hours a day. They drink very little. Instead, most of the moisture they need comes from their diet of eucalyptus leaves.

A newborn koala is tiny, about the size of a jelly bean. It is hairless, blind, and earless. As soon as it is born the baby koala crawls to its mother's pouch, where it continues to develop. After 6 months, the baby koala ventures out of its mother's pouch to eat eucalyptus leaves, but returns to her pouch to nurse. At about a year old, the young koala stops nursing and eats only leaves.

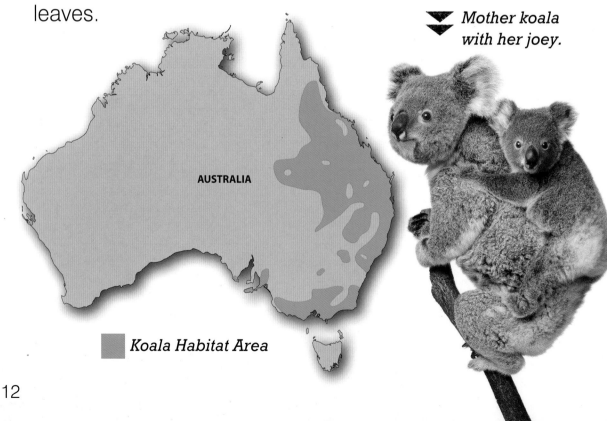

Mother koala with her joey.

AUSTRALIA

Koala Habitat Area

▼ *Koalas must watch out for predators such as dingoes, owls, and people.*

13

Koala Life Cycle:

1. A koala is born before it is completely formed. It is blind and cannot hear. It uses its strong front legs to crawl to its mother's pouch.

2. The baby koala, called a joey, stays inside its mother's pouch for 6 months, feeding on her milk and growing. At five months, the joey's eyes are open and it can survey the world from the safety of its mother's pouch.

3. At 6 months, the joey leaves its mother's pouch for the first time. When frightened, it dashes back to the safety of the pouch. It continues to nurse and sleep in the pouch.

4. At 9 months, a baby koala is too big for its mother's pouch. It rides on her back, holding on with a tight grip.

5. At a year old, a koala stops drinking its mother's milk and eats only eucalyptus leaves. It is ready to leave its mother and go off on its own.

6. At 2 years old, female koalas are ready to breed. Males are ready at 4 years. Koalas live up to 12 years in the wild.

The Virginia opossum is the only marsupial native to North America. About the size of a large house cat, the opossum has gray fur, a long nose, and a hairless, **prehensile** tail. It uses its tail to grasp onto tree limbs and can even hang upside down for short periods of time. Opossums live in deciduous forests, open woods, and farmland. **Omnivores**, they eat both plants and animals, including grubs, eggs, flowers, and fruit. They are also scavengers, and eat garbage and other dead animals.

Virginia opossums live in forests, woods, and farmland of the United States, Mexico, and Central America.

NORTH
AMERICA

Opossum Habitat Area

Playing Possum

When an opossum feels threatened, it rolls on its side and pretends to be dead. It can lie still for up to 6 hours, eyes and mouth open, waiting for its predators to lose interest and walk away. Sometimes it emits a foul odor for added effect.

Chapter 4
Threats

Koalas and Tasmanian devils are threatened by habitat destruction, traffic deaths, disease, and attacks by dogs. Loss of habitat occurs when humans cut down trees to make way for farming and building. When families move into newly-built neighborhoods they bring pets, including dogs, that attack koalas and Tasmanian devils still living in nearby woods.

Threats to kangaroos come from the dingo, the wedge-tailed eagle, and humans. Dingoes are wild dogs that live in Australia. They usually hunt small animals, but, when necessary, they work together in packs to take down sheep and kangaroos. Humans consider the red kangaroo a pest, and hunt it for its meat and skin.

Dingoes

Common wombats have rear-facing pouches that keep the dirt away from their babies when they tunnel underground.

Wombats and sugar gliders face threats related to habitat loss. Using forests and grasslands for development leaves them with fewer places to live.

Sugar gliders spread out the flap of skin between their fifth finger and their ankle and glide from tree to tree. They love to dine on insects, nectar, pollen, and small animals.

Marsupial babies are tiny at birth. As they grow and develop in their mother's pouch, they become climbers, gliders, and hoppers, ready to take on the exciting world that awaits them.

Glossary

carcasses (KAR-kuhss-uz): the bodies of dead animals

carnivores (KAR-nuh-vorz): animals that eat only meat

gestation (jess-TAY-shuhn): the time an animal spends developing inside its mother's womb

herbivores (HUR-buh-vorz): animals that eat only plants

mammals (MAM-uhlz): warm-blooded animals that produce milk to feed their young

migrate (MYE-grate): change habitat or location

nocturnal (nok-TUR-nuhl): active at night

omnivores (OM-nuh-vorz): animals that eat both plants and meat

prehensile (pree-HEN-sihl): adapted for grabbing or holding on to something

scavengers (SCAV-uhn-jurz): animals that eat dead animals and rotting plants

Index

Websites To Visit

www.australian-animals.net/

www.kidport.com/reflib/science/animals/marsupials.htm

www.planetozkids.com/oban/animals/facts-koala.htm

About the Author

Jeanne Sturm lives in Florida with her husband, Kurt, and children, David, Krista, and Robert. She enjoys reading, bicycling, and windsurfing. Although she's never seen a marsupial in the wild, she does enjoy spotting deer, alligators, and hawks in the conservation area near her home.

Ask The Author!
www.rem4students.com